Baptism and the Lord's Supper

The Gospel Coalition Booklets
Edited by D. A. Carson & Timothy Keller

Gospel-Centered Ministry *by D. A. Carson and Timothy Keller*

The Restoration of All Things *by Sam Storms*

The Church: God's New People *by Tim Savage*

Creation *by Andrew M. Davis*

The Holy Spirit *by Kevin L. DeYoung*

What Is the Gospel? *by Bryan Chapell*

The Plan *by Colin S. Smith*

Can We Know the Truth? *by Richard D. Phillips*

Sin and the Fall *by Reddit Andrews III*

Christ's Redemption *by Sandy Willson*

Justification *by Philip Graham Ryken*

The Gospel and Scripture: How to Read the Bible *by Mike Bullmore*

The Kingdom of God *by Stephen Um*

Baptism and the Lord's Supper

*Thabiti Anyabwile &
J. Ligon Duncan*

WHEATON, ILLINOIS

Baptism and the Lord's Supper

Copyright © 2011 by The Gospel Coalition

Published by Crossway
    1300 Crescent Street
    Wheaton, Illinois 60187

All rights reserved. No part of this publication may be reproduced, stored in a retrieval system, or transmitted in any form by any means, electronic, mechanical, photocopy, recording, or otherwise, without the prior permission of the publisher, except as provided for by USA copyright law.

Cover design: Matthew Wahl

First printing 2011

Printed in the United States of America

Unless otherwise indicated, Scripture references are taken from the Holy Bible, New International Version®. Copyright © 1973, 1978, 1984 Biblica. Used by permission of Zondervan. All rights reserved. The "NIV" and "New International Version" trademarks are registered in the United States Patent and Trademark Office by Biblica. Use of either trademark requires the permission of Biblica

Scripture quotations marked ESV are from the ESV® Bible (*The Holy Bible, English Standard Version*®), copyright © 2001 by Crossway. Used by permission. All rights reserved

Scripture quotations marked NASB are from *The New American Standard Bible*®. Copyright © The Lockman Foundation 1960, 1962, 1963, 1968, 1971, 1972, 1973, 1975, 1977, 1995. Used by permission.

All emphases in Scripture quotations have been added by the authors.

Trade paperback ISBN: 978-1-4335-2788-3

PDF ISBN: 978-1-4335-2789-0

Mobipocket ISBN: 978-1-4335-2790-6

ePub ISBN: 978-1-4335-2791-3

Crossway is a publishing ministry of Good News Publishers.

VP		20	19	18	17	16	15	14	13	12	11
14	13	12	11	10	9	8	7	6	5	4	3	2	1

Contents

Baptism   8
The Lord's Supper   18

We believe that baptism and the Lord's Supper are ordained by the Lord Jesus himself. The former is connected with entrance into the new-covenant community, the latter with ongoing covenant renewal. Together they are simultaneously God's pledge to us, divinely ordained means of grace, our public vows of submission to the once crucified and now resurrected Christ, and anticipations of his return and of the consummation of all things.

—The Gospel Coalition Statement of Faith

[Anyabwile] sat across the table with Matthew, a creative, inquisitive, free-spirited twenty-five-year-old. He'd come into the restaurant as breezy and bright as the warm Caribbean day outside. Just a few minutes late, he smiled and casually apologized for any inconvenience he'd caused.

Taking up our menus, I wondered to myself what lay ahead in our conversation. Though he'd been attending church for nearly a year, I wasn't sure exactly where Matthew was spiritually or what his questions for me would be. No sooner had we ordered our meals and returned the menus to our waitress then Matthew turned to me and said, "So, I have a lot of questions."

"Wonderful," I replied, relieved that I wouldn't have to drag any conversation out of my young friend. "What's on your mind?"

That day Matthew asked me lots of things. Many of his questions dealt with themes such as God's glory and anger with sinners, the reliability of the Bible, the resurrection, the exclusivity of Jesus, and the future. For nearly two hours we enjoyed a really wonderful exploration of the Bible's teachings on these topics.

But near the end of our conversation, I grew concerned that Matthew, while asking great theological questions, was failing to deal with the more personal heart of the matter. So I asked, "Matthew, what will you do about your sin?"

He gulped, slightly taken aback, and replied, "I hope Jesus has taken care of them." Then he proceeded to tell me how six months earlier he had come to accept Christ as his Savior and Lord. At the end of his story, he said, "I want to join the church, but I'm not ready to be baptized."

Matthew had come to a point many Christians sometimes reach. He had come to understand the gospel and to rely upon Jesus for his salvation, but he had not yet come to understand just what that had to do with the local church. In other words, he had not come to see that the Lord gave two ordinances or sacraments for marking both his initiation into the Christian life and his ongoing fellowship with Christ. In giving these ordinances to the church, the Lord provided "visible words" that communicate the believer's union with Christ in his death, burial, and resurrection (baptism) and the outworking of that union, namely, continuing fellowship with the Lord (the Lord's Supper). Both, then, become not just ordinances to be obeyed but also means of grace for our strengthening and enjoyment until Christ returns.

Baptism

I live in a country where many people have come to believe that only the "near perfect Christian" may be baptized. Some have come to attach so much importance to baptism that the ordinance no longer applies to the "regular Christian" who experiences imperfection and struggles with sin. They assume that delaying baptism is the appropriate path for most Christians. During our lunch, Matthew expressed these beliefs.

I realize that Christians in many other places in the world make precisely the opposite error. They assign very little importance to baptism. Baptism may be a rite you undertake "when you're old enough" or an unimportant exercise left optional to each believer. It's a box checked off the spiritual to-do list and basically forgotten.

Christians may fall into either error: assigning either too little or too much importance to baptism. In doing so, we risk losing the beauty and richness of a command that Jesus himself instituted and that Christian churches have celebrated for nearly two thousand years. The solution is to embrace a biblical understanding of baptism that immerses us deeply in the gracious and efficacious work of our Lord Jesus Christ on behalf of sinners.

What Is Baptism?

In the most basic terms, baptism is a sign and a seal. As the Westminster Confession of Faith puts it, baptism "is a sign and seal of the covenant of grace, of [the believer's] ingrafting into Christ, of regeneration, of remission of sins, and of his giving up unto God, through Jesus Christ, to walk in newness of life" (28.1).

A sign is a symbol pointing to a greater reality or idea. Baptism is "a neon light flashing 'Gospel, Gospel, Gospel.'"[1] When the church practices baptism, she testifies to the death, burial, and resurrection of Jesus Christ and signifies the sinner's union with Christ in all he did and accomplished on our behalf.

But baptism (and the Lord' Supper too, for that matter) is also a seal:

> The sacraments are not only signs that point our attention back to Jesus Christ as presented in the gospel and thus remind us of his grace offered to the whole world. They are also seals, which assure us that God's grace and promise are given to us in particular. This word "seal," when used in the context of the Reformation, referred to the wax imprint that marked a document as official and legally binding. In this context, Baptism is the seal whereby God takes the general promise of the gospel and applies it to us in particular. In the ancient world, the same word also referred to marks on the body—brands or tattoos which functioned as a mark of ownership. We are "marked" by Christ's death and resurrection, as witnessed both by baptism and the Lord's Supper.[2]

A ruler or king might affix his seal to an official edict or law. Correspondence received from a magistrate or influential person would bear the imprint or seal belonging to his office or family. Or a slave might bear the markings of his owner. Recipients and the public would thereby recognize the bearer of such a seal or marking as belonging to its owner.

In baptism, God places his mark upon the one baptized. The repentant and professing Christian receives the seal of heaven's ownership. God speaks to us in baptism: "This one so marked or sealed belongs to me."

In modern evangelicalism, people often speak of making a "public profession of faith." That phrase has come to be associated with things such as responding to altar calls, praying certain prayers, or signing response cards. In general, these actions focus on what we say to God. Unfortunately, many of these practices leave us thinking solely about what we say, not realizing that God wishes to speak of his love to his people. And they make what we say the decisive action or speech. But the Bible strongly supports none of those practices. The apostles and the early church, however, did have a way for repentant sinners to make a public profession, to signify their faith in Christ while receiving the seal of God's salvation—baptism.

The Beauty of Baptism

The beauty of baptism may be observed by considering what baptism signifies, for baptism wonderfully associates the believer with the many riches found in Christ.

The Atonement of Christ

First, baptism visibly portrays the atonement that Jesus accomplished. Redemption and the remission of sins are central to Christ's work and therefore central to the meaning of baptism:

> When you were dead in your sins and in the uncircumcision of your sinful nature, God made you alive with Christ. He forgave us all our sins, having canceled the written code, with its regulations, that was against us and that stood opposed to us; he took it away, nailing it to the cross. And having disarmed the powers and authorities, he made a public spectacle of them, triumphing over them by the cross. (Col. 2:13–15)

In baptism, we are reminded of our Lord's own baptism on our behalf. The Savior taught, "I have a baptism to be baptized with, and how great is my distress until it is accomplished" (Luke 12:50 ESV). When overly ambitious disciples requested to sit at his side in his kingdom, Jesus humbled them by replying, "You do not know what you are asking. Are you able to drink the cup that I drink, or to be baptized with the baptism with which I am baptized?" (Mark 10:38 ESV). The cup the Master drank was the cup of the Father's wrath against sin. The distressing baptism he endured was the baptism of the cross where he made propitiation for the sins of the world (1 John 2:2).

Baptism reminds the church and the individual Christian of Jesus' cross, where Jesus took away and nailed our sins and where Jesus' triumph becomes our triumph. Baptism reminds us that Christ has suffered our judgment and made peace with God for us.

Union with Christ

Second, baptism represents the sinner's spiritual union with Jesus in his death, burial, and resurrection.

> What shall we say, then? Shall we go on sinning so that grace may increase? By no means! We died to sin; how can we live in it any longer?

Baptism and the Lord's Supper

Or don't you know that all of us who were baptized into Christ Jesus were baptized into his death? We were therefore buried with him through baptism into death in order that, just as Christ was raised from the dead through the glory of the Father, we too may live a new life. If we have been united with him like this in his death, we will certainly also be united with him in his resurrection. (Rom. 6:1–5)

When Jesus died, we died with him. When he was buried, we were buried. When he rose, we rose, too! Because we are united to Christ by faith, we receive the benefits of Jesus' life, death, and resurrection. Through faith we vicariously participate in all that Jesus did. Baptism pictures that spiritual reality.

Our union with Christ is so strong that some have compared baptism to marriage. For example, Marion Clark writes, "God is our bridegroom, who has chosen us, paid the dowry, and given us his ring so that all may know that we belong to him. Even more, he has done so to make clear to us that we are his. The ceremony of baptism asserts that his love for us is not a dream but a reality."[3] In baptism we exchange vows uniting Christ, the bridegroom, to his bride, the church.

Union with the Church

Baptism not only pictures our union with Christ but also our union with his body, the church. Having been joined to Christ through faith and the operation of the Holy Spirit, by the same Spirit "we were all baptized by one Spirit into one body" (1 Cor. 12:13). Or as the apostle Paul writes elsewhere, "There is one body and one Spirit—just as you were called to one hope when you were called—one Lord, one faith, one baptism; one God and Father of all, who is over all and through all and in all" (Eph. 4:4–6).

Baptized individuals profess that they are joined to Christ's body through faith. That union with Christ manifests itself in union with his people, most concretely demonstrated by commitment and membership in a local church.

Whenever a couple has a new baby, family and friends visit the hospital, deliver well wishes, and rejoice at the addition of this new life. In a similar way, when people receive the sign and seal of baptism, they become a part of God's family, the church. They enjoy the privileges and responsibilities of family membership. Don Whitney explains this well: "When God brings a person into spiritual life, that person enters into the spiritual and invisible body of Christ—the universal church. When that spiritual experience is pictured in water baptism, that is the individual's symbolic entry into the tangible and visible body of Christ—the local church."[4]

Consecration to God

Finally, we should understand that baptism signifies our consecration to God. In baptism we are set apart for worship and service to the God of our salvation. We are marked out from the world and sealed as belonging to God. This is why the apostle Paul often writes of New Testament ethical requirements when discussing baptism. For example:

> In him you were also circumcised, in the putting off of the sinful nature, not with a circumcision done by the hands of men but with the circumcision done by Christ, having been buried with him in baptism and raised with him through your faith in the power of God, who raised him from the dead. (Col. 2:11–12)

> In the same way, count yourselves dead to sin but alive to God in Christ Jesus. Therefore do not let sin reign in your mortal body so that you obey its evil desires. Do not offer the parts of your body to sin, as instruments of wickedness, but rather offer yourselves to God, as those who have been brought from death to life; and offer the parts of your body to him as instruments of righteousness. For sin shall not be your master, because you are not under law, but under grace. (Rom. 6:11–14)

Because our lives are united with Christ by faith and the Spirit's engrafting, we are obligated to live "circumcised" lives, to "put off the sinful nature." We "count ourselves dead to sin but alive to God in Christ Jesus" and we "offer ourselves to God." Because we died with Christ, sin no longer reigns over us. We are freed from the tyranny of unrighteousness. "Our old self was crucified with him so that the body of sin might be done away with, that we should no longer be slaves to sin" (Rom. 6:6). We belong to a new Master. Credobaptists would add that we go down to the "watery grave" to be raised in newness of life.[5]

Baptism and the Lord's Supper

Our baptism obligates us to live in righteousness so that we honor, not shame, our Lord with whom we have been buried and raised to life in baptism. We cannot go back. We have entered into the new covenant; we have sworn allegiance to our king. Now we must live as citizens and servants of his kingdom.[6]

My friend Matthew did not see the beauty of baptism. He thought of baptism primarily as something he said to the world: "Hey, I'm living for Jesus and plan not to mess up." He failed to recognize that God says in baptism, "Hey, you belong to me. I've made you new. You will live for me because I will live in you."

When viewed from that perspective, baptism gains the beauty and importance it deserves. It becomes a means of grace for the believer, a reminder of the gospel and Savior that rescue us.

Moreover, baptism opens the doors of continuing fellowship with our Lord. That continuing fellowship with the Lord finds expression in another sign and seal, the Lord's Supper or Communion Meal.

Paedobaptists and Credobaptists

I [Duncan] love the way Thabiti lays out the doctrine of baptism here and the pastoral view he gives us of its importance in the lives of Christians. He, as a Baptist, and I, as a Presbyterian, thus far agree. But we also want to acknowledge that there are some areas of significant disagreement among otherwise united members of The Gospel Coalition on the subject of baptism. In general, we agree on the meaning, importance, and function of baptism, but we have some disagreements on the mode and subjects (or proper recipients of baptism). These differences are not inconsequential, and so we want to honor one another's consciences under the Word of God, and we want the members of our respective churches to understand and take these issues seriously.[7]

Some of us in The Gospel Coalition are credobaptists (that is, Christians like Thabiti who believe that only believers should be baptized) and others of us are paedobaptists (that is, Christians like me who believe that both believers and their children should be baptized). Both groups seek to ground their baptismal practice in the teaching of Scripture, but both come to different conclusions as to what the Bible teaches about the proper recipients of baptism.

Evangelical paedobaptists believe that the Bible teaches that the church should baptize the children of believers as well as adult professing believers who have not been previously baptized. We believe that baptism is a new-covenant sign that points to and confirms the gracious saving promise of God to his people and its fulfillment in Jesus Christ. We base the administration of baptism to believers and their children on our understanding of passages such as Genesis 17, Matthew 28, Colossians 2, 1 Corinthians 7, and Acts 2 and 16.

We agree with our credobaptist friends that (1) Christ commands Christian baptism in Matthew 28 ("Go... make disciples... baptizing ... and ... teaching them") and that (2) believers should be baptized as in Acts 8:

> Then Philip opened his mouth, and beginning with this Scripture he preached Jesus to him. As they went along the road they came to some water; and the eunuch said, "Look! Water! What prevents me from being baptized?" *And Philip said, "If you believe with all your heart, you may." And he answered and said, "I believe that Jesus Christ is the Son of God."* And he ordered the chariot to stop; and they both went down into the water, Philip as well as the eunuch, and he baptized him. (vv. 35–38 NASB)

But we disagree on a third point, because paedobaptists also believe that Christian believers *and their children* should be baptized. If we had to reduce our biblical argument for paedobaptism to one (albeit complex!) sentence, it would be something like this:

> God made promises to believers and their children in both the Old and Testaments, attached signs to those promises in both the Old and New Testaments, explicitly required the sign of initiation into his family (circumcision) to be applied to believers and their children in the Old Testament, and implicitly appointed the new-covenant sign of initiation (baptism) to be given to believers and their children in the New Testament.

Credobaptists disagree and argue not only that paedobaptists misunderstand the passages that we appeal to, but also that the New Testament references to baptism entail a command to baptize only those who profess personal faith in Jesus Christ (e.g., Acts 2:41; 8:12;

Baptism and the Lord's Supper

10:44-48; Rom. 6:3-4; Gal. 3:27). They hold that passages such as Jeremiah 31 teach that the church, under the terms of the new covenant, is the gathered assembly of *believing* disciples, and that in this respect they differ from believers under the old covenant, which clearly included children.

Paedobaptists, on the other hand, believe that the membership of the local church is made up of believers and their children, and that in this respect the new covenant does not differ from the old covenant. Hence, a difference in ecclesiology (the doctrine of the church) is one of the main factors in the credobaptist and paedobaptist disagreement over the proper recipients of baptism.

A slightly less significant disagreement concerns the mode of baptism. Credobaptists generally argue that baptism is to be performed only by immersion or dipping a person into water. They also typically hold that the mode is so bound up with Jesus' command that those who are not immersed are not baptized. Meanwhile, most paedobaptists believe that baptism is best done by affusion (pouring or sprinkling water upon the recipient) but that mode is not of the essence of the rite; thus, immersion is a valid, but not a required, mode of baptism.

Those who argue for immersion do so on a number of grounds. They assert that the Greek word for baptism means "immersion," that the examples of baptism in the New Testament (e.g., Matt. 3:16; Mark 1:5, 10; John 3:23; Acts 8:36-38) indicate that immersion was the mode, that Paul teaches immersion in his explanation of baptism in Romans 6:1-11 (cf. Col. 2:11-12), and that passages adduced by paedobaptists as examples of nonimmersion are unconvincing.

Those who argue for affusion argue that there are places in the biblical usage of baptism where it cannot mean "to immerse" (e.g., Lev. 14:6, 51; Acts 1:5; 1 Cor. 10:2; Heb. 9:10-23); that only one passage in the New Testament actually describes the mode of baptism (Acts 1-2) and that all the rest describe merely the location of baptism (Matthew 3; Mark 1; Acts 8), not its mode of administration; that there are places in the New Testament where immersion is unlikely or impossible (Acts 9:17-18; 10:47; 16:32-33); and above all that water baptism signifies the baptism of the Holy Spirit, which is depicted only by pouring out, not immersion (see Acts 1:4-5; 2:2-3; cf. Matt. 3:11; Luke 3:16; Acts 11:15-16).

Despite these important and ongoing differences, both sides are able to affirm Article 12 of The Gospel Coalition Confessional Statement. Furthermore, we also stand with one another in rejecting baptismal regeneration. This view, held by Roman Catholics, Eastern Orthodox, High Anglicans or Anglo-Catholics, Lutherans, and groups such as the Church of Christ, is that water baptism is "the instrumental cause of regeneration, and that the grace of regeneration is effectually conveyed through the administration of that rite wherever duly performed."[8]

Without in any way diminishing the importance of baptism or its necessity for Christian obedience, we deny that water baptism regenerates or that it causes the new birth. In the Bible, uniformly, covenant signs, sacraments, or ordinances (as many of our Baptist friends prefer) signify and confirm the spiritual realities that they represent; they do not produce those realities.

This is precisely Paul's point in Romans 4:1–12 about Abraham's circumcision. Abraham was not justified *by* his circumcision but *before* his circumcision, and God gave the covenant sign of circumcision to confirm, not to confer, Abraham's justification (Genesis 15) before he was ever circumcised (Genesis 17). So we agree with the Puritan theologian Stephen Charnock, who says that regeneration

> is not external baptism. Many men take their baptism for regeneration. The ancients usually give it this term. One calls our Saviour's baptism his regeneration. This confers not grace, but engageth to it: outward water cannot convey inward life. How can water, a material thing, work upon the soul in a spiritual manner? Neither can it be proved, that ever the Spirit of God is tied to any promise, to apply himself to the soul in a gracious operation, when water is applied to the body. If it were so, that all that were baptized, were regenerate; then all that were baptized would be saved; or else the doctrine of perseverance falls to the ground. Baptism is a mean of conveying this grace, when the Spirit is pleased to operate with it. But it doth not work as a physical cause upon the soul, as a purge doth upon the humours of the body: for it is the sacrament of regeneration, as the Lord's Supper is of nourishment. As a man cannot be said to be nourished without faith, so he cannot be said to be a new creature without faith. Put the most delicious meat into the mouth of a dead man, you do not nourish him, because he wants a principle of life to concoct and digest it. Faith alone is the principle of spiritual life, and

the principle draws nourishment from the means of God's appointment. Some indeed say, that regeneration is conferred in baptism upon the elect, and exerts itself afterwards in conversion. But how so active a principle as spiritual life should lie dead, and asleep so long, even many years which intervene between baptism and conversion is not easily conceivable.[9]

Very often Christians who deny the doctrine of baptismal regeneration are accused of reducing baptism to a "bare sign," that is, making it an empty symbol that "does nothing." But this is not the case. Baptism is God's means not to regenerate or justify us but to confirm his promise to us, put his mark on us, and assure us of his love, all of which serve to increase and strengthen the faith of the believer and thus promote our growth in grace.

This is why the Westminster Larger Catechism urges believers to "improve their baptism" every time they see baptism administered to another. What did those theologians mean by exhorting us to improve our baptism? To improve our baptism means to meditate on its blessings, to make use of it, to take full advantage of it, and to gain the maximum benefit from it as a means of growing in grace, especially when we are present at its administration in public worship. The Larger Catechism says:

> The needful but much neglected duty of improving our Baptism, is to be performed by us all our life long, especially in the time of temptation, and when we are present at the administration of it to others; by serious and thankful consideration of the nature of it, and of the ends for which Christ instituted it, the privileges and benefits conferred and sealed thereby, and our solemn vow made therein; by being humbled for our sinful defilement, our falling short of, and walking contrary to, the grace of baptism, and our engagements; by growing up to assurance of pardon of sin, and of all other blessings sealed to us in that sacrament; by drawing strength from the death and resurrection of Christ, into whom we are baptized, for the mortifying of sin, and quickening of grace; and by endeavoring to live by faith, to have our conversation in holiness and righteousness, as those that have therein given up their names to Christ; and to walk in brotherly love, as being baptized by the same Spirit into one body.[10]

On this paedobaptists and credobaptists heartily agree.

The Lord's Supper

I [Anyabwile] remember my wedding day as though it were yesterday. It was a very humid August day (the 31st, in case my wife reads this). We were married in my mother-in-law's front yard wearing traditional African clothing, and a small group of family and close friends attended. Our wedding marked the beginning of a joyful married life full of grace and love.

If baptism is akin to the believer's wedding-day union with Christ, then the Lord's Supper represents the ongoing renewal of love and vows sometimes celebrated at wedding anniversaries. I like the analogy. It reminds us that the Lord's Supper is far more than mere necessity, though it is necessary; far more than a mere memorial, though it reminds of precious things from redemptive history; and far more than mere ritual, though practiced by Christian churches of nearly every variety since the days of Jesus himself. The Lord's Supper, like a nightly dinner I share with my wife, or the occasional special days we observe together, provides an ongoing means of grace and fellowship between the Lord Jesus and his bride, the church.

When Did the Lord's Supper Get Its Start?

The Lord Jesus Christ himself instituted what many commonly call the Lord's Supper. The Lord's Supper, a name taken from the apostle Paul in 1 Corinthians 11:20, is also known as the Eucharist (1 Cor. 11:24) and Holy Communion (1 Cor. 10:16). While the name varies, each of the Synoptic Gospels records for us that amazing night when Jesus recast a centuries-old Jewish religious meal, the Passover, in terms of a new-covenant relationship with him accomplished by his death, burial, and resurrection (Matt. 26:26–30; Mark 14:22–26; Luke 22:19–20).

In the final plague on Egypt, God sent the angel of death to pass over the entire land, killing the firstborn male of every household and all livestock. To escape this judgment, Israelites were commanded to sacrifice an unblemished lamb for each household and to smear blood from the sacrifice on the doorposts of their homes. When the angel of death saw a home with sacrificial blood over its doorposts, he "passed over" that home. The blood turned away the judgment of God from that

Baptism and the Lord's Supper

home. During the exodus, God commanded Israel to commemorate their flight and deliverance from Egypt with a special meal (Exodus 12). For centuries after that fearful night, faithful Jewish families ate the Passover meal and explained the extraordinary deliverance of God to the next generation of Jewish children. No doubt Jesus' disciples had these things in mind when Jesus instructed them to prepare for the Passover (Matt. 26:17-19). But during that Passover meal, Jesus spoke remarkable and surprising words about the true meaning of the meal itself:

> Now as they were eating, Jesus took bread, and after blessing it broke it and gave it to the disciples, and said, "Take, eat; this is my body." And he took a cup, and when he had given thanks he gave it to them, saying, "Drink of it, all of you, for this is my blood of the covenant, which is poured out for many for the forgiveness of sins. I tell you I will not drink again of this fruit of the vine until that day when I drink it new with you in my Father's kingdom." (Matt. 26:26-29 ESV)

What Does the Lord's Supper Signify?

Like baptism, the Lord's Supper is a sign and a seal of God's grace. It, too, points to the gospel of our Lord, his sacrifice on our behalf, and redemption through faith in his name.

The Elements: Body and Blood

The night that Jesus instituted Holy Communion, he redefined the elements of the meal. The bread and wine stood for centuries as reminders of the lambs slaughtered on that first Passover. But Jesus revealed what even that first Passover signified: his body broken and his blood shed for sin. In the simple act of eating and drinking, the disciples were to remember that Christ our Passover Lamb was sacrificed (1 Cor. 5:7). He sacrificed himself "for many for the forgiveness of sins."

These signs, then, picture the gospel for the believing and the witnessing communities. When my young friend Matthew is baptized into the covenant community, he will gain the privilege of joining those who "proclaim the Lord's death until he comes" (1 Cor. 11:26). The Lord's Supper sensorially proclaims, enacts, and celebrates what is "of first importance . . . : that Christ died for our sins in accordance with the Scriptures" (1 Cor. 15:3 ESV).

Believers should never move far from appropriating the gospel benefits of Christ. So Christ grants the church signs or visible words that continually refresh our memories of his sacrifice. We eat and drink in faith, and our forgiveness through Christ is presented to us again as a reminder of the efficacy of his atonement.

The Meal: Nourishment

Perhaps the most obvious thing that the Lord's Supper signifies is the spiritual nourishment that believers receive at the meal. Just as actual food and wine nourish and please the body, the Communion meal nourishes and pleases the believer's soul. At the Communion Table we "take and eat," and "we drink the cup." We feed upon Christ by faith. The London Baptist Confession of Faith (1689) describes this view:

> Worthy receivers, outwardly partaking of the visible elements in this ordinance, do then also inwardly by faith, really and indeed, yet not carnally and corporally, but spiritually receive, and feed upon Christ crucified, and all the benefits of his death; the body and blood of Christ being then not corporally or carnally, but spiritually present to the faith of believers in that ordinance, as the elements themselves are to their outward senses. (30.7)

In this way, Jesus continues to be the food that nourishes Christians. He presents himself to our senses as "the bread of life." In feeding upon Christ by faith, we take into ourselves the benefits and grace that sustain us through the Christian life. "Jesus Christ is there offered to us in order that we may possess him, and in him all the fullness of grace which we can desire, and that herein we have a good aid to confirm our consciences in the faith which we ought to have in him."[11]

This means, in part, that the Lord's Supper belongs to the weak Christian. No one comes to the Table in unblemished worthiness or undiminished strength. We come to the Table in need. We come to the Table fresh from battles with sin, discouragement, unbelief, and the world. We need to be fed again. We need to receive the sustenance that Christ affords. By faith we receive the nourishment we need as we imbibe the benefits of Jesus' atoning work for sinners and weaklings.

Baptism and the Lord's Supper

The Administration: Participation with Christ

Not only are the elements of the Eucharist symbolic, but also the very administration or partaking of the Supper signifies important realities. Richard Phillips summarizes what the act of eating and drinking the Supper denotes:

> The eating of the elements by believers signifies their participation in the crucified Christ. Additionally, the partaking of the sacrament signifies the effect of Christ's death in giving life and strength to the soul, as food and drink sustain the body. Furthermore, just as the sacrament symbolizes the believers' union with Christ, it also places a visible difference between members of Christ's church and the world, while signifying believers' communion one to another in him.[12]

Phillips paraphrases well what the apostle Paul wrote centuries ago about the Eucharist:

> Therefore, my dear friends, flee from idolatry. I speak to sensible people; judge for yourselves what I say. Is not the cup of thanksgiving for which we give thanks a participation in the blood of Christ? And is not the bread that we break a participation in the body of Christ? (1 Cor. 10:14–16)

Eating and drinking this meal indicates the believer's union or participation with Christ. Believers thus appropriate the benefits of Jesus' atoning work and rely upon the continuing sustenance of Christ, the bread of life.

> This is the wonderful exchange which, out of his measureless benevolence, he has made with us; that, becoming Son of man with us, he has made us sons of God with him; that, by his descent to earth, he has prepared an ascent to heaven for us; that, by taking on our mortality, he has conferred his immortality upon us; that, accepting our weakness, he has strengthened us by his power; that, receiving our poverty unto himself, he has transferred his wealth to us; that, taking the weight of our iniquity upon himself (which oppressed us), he has clothed us with his righteousness.[13]

The Loaf: The Unity of the Church

Finally, the Lord's Supper also represents the unity of his people. "Because there is one loaf, we, who are many, are one body, for we all partake of the one loaf" (1 Cor. 10:17). When the church gathers at the Lord's Table, believers must recognize this profound spiritual unity. Paul chided the Corinthians for failing to reflect their unity in Christ. He had no praise for them, saying that their "meetings do more harm than good" (1 Cor. 11:17). The troubled divisions in the Corinthian church were manifested in divisions at the Lord's Table of all places (1 Cor. 1:10–13; 11:18–19). Selfishness and gluttony so prevailed at the Table that Paul concluded that it was "not the Lord's Supper you eat" (1 Cor. 11:20).

For the meal to truly be the Lord's Supper, members of the church needed to eat and drink in a worthy manner, in part by "recognizing the body of the Lord" at the Supper (1 Cor. 11:27, 29). That is, they were to recognize the unity of the church as one loaf, one people, joined together with Christ through his sacrifice on our behalf. Failure to do so constituted "sinning against the body and blood of the Lord" (1 Cor. 11:27). In such cases, the Table also became a place of judgment and self-examination (1 Cor. 11:28–34).

The Lord's Supper Is a Seal

But the Lord's Supper is not just a sign. Holy Communion is also a seal. By participating regularly in the Lord's Supper, Christians receive by faith the seal or "tattoo" that identifies them as belonging to Jesus and the covenant people of God. This is what is meant, in part, when The Gospel Coalition's Confessional Statement describes the Lord's Supper as "ongoing covenant renewal." In the Lord's Supper, the Lord speaks to his people of his ongoing love and mercy toward them.

> The Lord's Supper seals God's people by giving them a reliable attestation of their participation in Christ. It is Christ who thus identifies his own, stretching forth his hand to give them the bread and the cup of his covenant meal. John Murray says: "When we partake of the cup in faith, it is the Lord's own certification to us that all that the new covenant in his blood involves is ours. It is the seal of his grace and faithfulness."[14]

While baptism represents a kind of "I do" between Christ and his bride, the Supper repeats an "I continue" statement of love from Jesus to the church. Communion reminds us that his love endures forever.

The Lord's Supper and the Presence of Christ

If the Lord's Supper is an ongoing covenant renewal, then this suggests a genuine participation or communion with Christ. Jesus must be present at the Supper in a meaningful way. In the history of the church, there have been three major views on Christ's presence in the Lord's Supper.

Real Physical Presence

The Roman Catholic Church teaches that during the celebration of the Eucharist a miracle happens wherein the bread and wine continue to look like bread and wine but are really turned into the physical body and blood of Christ. This view, known as transubstantiation, also claims that in the Eucharist there is a re-presentation of Jesus' sacrifice on the cross, not just a sign remembering the Lord's death.

In arguing for transubstantiation, the Roman Catholic Church presses the metaphor of Jesus' words, "This is my body . . . this cup is my blood," into a woodenly literal straightjacket. Furthermore, their insistence that the Mass re-presents Jesus' sacrifice plainly contradicts the Bible (Rom. 6:10; Heb. 7:27; 9:12, 26; 10:10). Christ Jesus died once-for-all-time and now lives forever to intercede for his people.

The Lutheran view of Christ's presence in the Lord's Supper also takes the words of Christ's institution literally. But Luther maintained that the elements were not transformed; they remained bread and wine, but Jesus' body and blood are present in, under, and along with the elements of the sacrament. This view is called "consubstantiation."

Memorial View

On the other end of the spectrum there have been Christian bodies that deny that Christ is present in any way in the Lord's Supper. The memorial view emphasizes "Do this in remembrance of me" (1 Cor. 11:24–25). So the Supper becomes a remembrance or memorial. Many commonly associate this view with the Swiss Reformer Huldrych Zwingli, who opposed the Roman Catholic and Lutheran views of Christ's presence in the Supper.

Spiritual Presence

A third option holds that Christ—while not physically present—is present *spiritually* in Communion. The elements remain bread and wine, but by faith Christ meets with and communes with his people at the Supper.

The statements "This is my body" and "This cup is the new covenant in my blood" are figurative statements, according to the spiritual-presence view. The bread and wine do not change in any real way. Yet the Supper represents more than mere commemoration. In calling the statements figurative or symbolic, this view does not downplay the reality and importance of the thing signified. The Lord's Supper combines tremendous mystery and genuine spiritual blessing.

> Even though it seems unbelievable that Christ's flesh, separated from us by such great distance, penetrates to us, so that it becomes our food, let us remember how far the secret power of the Holy Spirit towers above all our senses, and how foolish it is to wish to measure his immeasurableness by our measure. What, then, our mind does not comprehend, let faith conceive: that the Spirit truly unites things separated in space.
>
> Now, that sacred partaking of his flesh and blood, by which Christ pours his life into us, as if it penetrated into our bones and marrow, he also testifies and seals in the Supper—not by presenting a vain and empty sign, but by manifesting there the effectiveness of his Spirit to fulfill what he promises. And truly he offers and shows the reality there signified to all who sit at that spiritual banquet, although it is received with benefit by believers alone, who accept such great generosity with true faith and gratefulness of heart.[15]

When we behold and partake of the elements in Communion, we receive by faith all that they signify regarding the broken body and shed blood of the Lord Jesus Christ. By faith, Christ joins us at the Supper, and we anticipate the day when faith gives way to sight and we eat with the Savior in the Father's kingdom (Matt. 26:29).

Baptism and the Lord's Supper

A Pastoral Hope

I look forward to the day when Matthew celebrates baptism with the church. I look forward to seeing Matthew rejoice to receive the sign and seal of his union with Christ through faith. And Lord willing, Matthew and the church will regularly come to the Lord's Supper to see and receive afresh the work of Christ and the benefits of his sacrifice. Together we will hear the Lord express his ownership of and love for us in the visible signs he gives to his church. We remember and proclaim together our Savior's sacrificial death for us even as we anticipate eating with him in the Father's kingdom. By these sacraments we receive fresh supplies of grace. By them we receive Christ our Lord and the joy of communing with him. What a wonderful joy to participate in these rich privileges given by Christ Jesus to his people!

Some Theological-Pastoral Reflections

[Duncan] Thabiti has beautifully, clearly, biblically, and pastorally outlined our understanding of the Lord's Supper, as well as outlined for us three of the main positions on how Christ is "present" (or not!) in the elements and/or the administration of them, but perhaps it would be helpful to summarize the emphases of the key scriptural passages on the sacraments or ordinances in general (e.g., Genesis 9; 12; 15; 17; Exodus 12; 24; Isaiah 7; Acts 2; Romans 4; 1 Cor. 1:17; 1 Pet. 3:18–22) and the Lord's Supper in particular (Matt. 26:17–29; Mark 14:12–25; Luke 22:7–23; 1 Cor. 11:17–32).[16]

This is important because the clearer that Christians are on what the Lord's Supper is and isn't, and what it does and doesn't do, and what it is and isn't for, the more helpful it will be to them as a means of growth.

1) Baptism and the Lord's Supper, as sacraments, or ordinances, or covenant signs/seals, do not inaugurate or effect a covenant relationship; rather, they represent and confirm a previously existing, election-originated, promise-commenced, grace-established, Father-initiated, Spirit-bestowed, Christ-grounded, faith-received, covenant relationship.
2) Baptism and the Lord's Supper, as sacraments/ordinances, are part of the divine program of assurance. They are given to buttress and grow faith in the covenantal promises of God. It is this area that relates to the idea of sacraments as seals.

3) God is not present "in" any sacrament, but the sacramental analogy in every sacrament points to the glorious, gracious, covenantal, communional, promise of the presence of God, and by the Spirit we know something of this presence. That is, through the sacrament, and especially through the ongoing and repeated Lord's Supper, we are pointed to and experience a foretaste of the glorious communion of the ultimate covenant promise, "I will be your God and you will be my people," and the ultimate covenant hope, "God with us," and the ultimate covenant fellowship, "to recline at his table."
4) There are objective and subjective aspects to the sacraments/ordinances, as well as inward and outward aspects. Any refusal to come to grips with the distinction between the sign (outward) and the thing signified (inward) overthrows the sacrament, as Calvin noted. Furthermore, the objective (the sign) exists for the subjective (the reality that is *sign*ified). So to talk about sacramental efficacy in the absence of the key subjective instrument (faith) and effects (strengthened faith, growth in grace, assurance) is to miss the whole point of the Spirit's use of and goal for the Lord's Supper.
5) Following on this, sacramental signs do not bestow the sacramental reality. The sacraments are efficacious in the sense that they accomplish God's purpose, but they are not invariably efficacious. There are always Ishmaels and Simons. Those who want an invariable objective efficacy, that is, those who want sacraments and ordinances to automatically bestow grace just by their being administered, will have to go to Rome or Constantinople, and without the slightest support from biblical covenant thought.
6) Not one of the Lord's Supper narratives focuses our attention on the bodily presence of Christ in the Supper. The language of body and blood clearly points us to contemplation of the covenantal sacrifice of Christ.[17]
7) Positively, the New Testament's Lord's Supper narratives press us (a) to give thanks to God for the salvation we have by Christ; (b) to commemorate Christ's death as the new-covenant exodus in a covenant meal; (c) to proclaim or set forth the incalculable significance and glorious meaning of his saving death; and (d) to commune with him and with his people, which is his body.

Paedo-Communion and a Parting Word

Though the practice of paedo-communion (communing infants and young children, apart from a credible profession of faith), long confined to Eastern Orthodoxy, has gained some currency in liberal and high-church Protestant circles (with a few minor exceptions in some conservative Reformed quadrants), most evangelical Protestant paedobaptists and credobaptists agree that the Lord's Table is only for those who are trusting in Jesus Christ. So the proper participants in the Lord's Supper are *those who trust in Jesus Christ alone for their salvation as he is offered in the gospel and who have received the sign of membership (baptism) in the body of Christ, his church.* The Lord's Supper is for professing believers in the Lord Jesus Christ who have "discerned the body of the Lord," that is, the church (1 Cor. 11:29).

In conclusion to our exposition of Article 12 of The Gospel Coalition Confessional Statement, it may be helpful to summarize some high points of the biblical teaching on the nature of the sacraments or ordinances. God's sacraments or covenant signs and seals are "visible words" (Augustine). In them, we see with our eyes the promise of God. Indeed, in the sacraments we see, smell, touch, and taste the word. In the public reading and preaching of Scripture, God addresses our mind and conscience through the hearing. In the sacraments, he uniquely addresses our mind and conscience through the other senses. God's promise is made tangible in, through, and to the senses. A sacrament is a covenant sign and seal, which means it reminds us and assures us of a promise. That is, it points to and confirms a gracious promise of God to his people.

Another way of saying it is that a sacrament is an action that God designed to sign (symbolize) and seal (ratify) a covenantal reality that the power and grace of God accomplished; the Word of God has communicated its significance, and people received or entered into its reality only by faith. Hence, the weakness and frailty of human faith welcomes this gracious act of reassurance. The sacraments by nature supplement and confirm God's promises in his Word, and the grace they convey is the same grace conveyed by preaching. The sacraments are efficacious for only the elect since their benefits sanctify them and are received by faith.

Notes

1. D. Marion Clark, "Baptism: Joyful Sign of the Gospel," in *Give Praise to God: A Vision for Reforming Worship*, ed. Philip Graham Ryken, Derek W. H. Thomas, and J. Ligon Duncan III (Phillipsburg, NJ: P&R, 2003), 171.
2. James V. Brownson, *The Promise of Baptism: An Introduction to Baptism in Scripture and the Reformed Tradition* (Grand Rapids, MI: Eerdmans, 2007), 24–25.
3. Clark, "Baptism," 179.
4. Donald S. Whitney, *Spiritual Disciplines within the Church* (Chicago: Moody, 1996), 138.
5. Obviously, Presbyterian paedobaptists do not draw the same conclusion from Romans 6 as to the mode of baptism (i.e., going down to "the watery grave") that credobaptists do, as explained below.
6. Clark, "Baptism," 177.
7. Of the writing and reading of books on baptism there is (it seems) no end. But here are a few of the very best credo- and paedobaptist presentations of the respective arguments that look at both Scripture and Christian history. (1) *Believer's Baptism: Sign of the New Covenant in Christ*, ed. Thomas R. Schreiner and Shawn D. Wright (Nashville, TN: Broadman, 2006); an impressive set of essays from noted credobaptist scholars. (2) *Baptism: Three Views*, ed. David F. Wright (Downers Grove, IL: InterVarsity, 2009). Professor Wright was my *Doktorvater* at the University of Edinburgh, and though a Church of Scotland (Presbyterian) elder, he was a convinced credobaptist and a formidable student of the history of infant baptism. This book has strong credo and paedo presentations, as well as a Bunyan-style compromise view. (3) George R. Beasley-Murray, *Baptism in the New Testament* (London: Macmillan, 1962); an exhaustive, scholarly study that argues the believers-only baptism view. (4) Geoffrey Bromiley, *Children of Promise: The Case for Baptizing Infants* (Grand Rapids, MI: Eerdmans, 1979). Bromiley was a noted historical theological, and though small and meant for a popular audience, this little book is an able presentation of the paedobaptist view. (5) Paul K. Jewett, *Infant Baptism and the Covenant of Grace* (Grand Rapids, MI: Eerdmans, 1978). A critique of infant baptism from a covenantal believers baptism position. (6) *The Case for Covenantal Infant Baptism*, ed. Gregg Strawbridge (Phillipsburg, NJ: P&R, 2003); a collection of essays arguing the paedobaptist view ably. (7) Rowland Ward, *Baptism in Scripture and History* (Melbourne: New Melbourne Press, 1991); a brief, but helpful presentation of the issues from a paedobaptist perspective that focuses on mode. (8) Joachim Jeremias, *Infant Baptism in the First Four Centuries* (London: SCM, 1960); a survey of the Patristic evidence, asserting a paedobaptist interpretation of the material. (9) Kurt Aland, *Did the Early Church Baptize Infants?* (Philadelphia: Westminster, 1963); a credobaptist rejoinder to Jeremias by a noted scholar. (10) Joachim Jeremias, *The Origins of Infant Baptism: A Further Study in Reply to Kurt Aland* (London: SCM, 1963). Jeremias responds to Aland, still advocating a paedobaptist interpretation of the Patristic data. (11) Everett Ferguson, *Baptism in the Early Church: History, Theology and Liturgy in the First Five Centuries* (Grand Rapids, MI: Eerdmans, 2009). A noted scholar of Patristics, out of the Campbellite tradition, presents a massive survey of the evidence from the church Fathers. He concludes, mode: immersion; purpose: forgiveness and regeneration (at least from Tertullian on). Needless to say, both credobaptist and paedobaptist members of The Gospel Coalition would draw different conclusions from the evidence, but Ferguson's work is important.
8. James Orr, "Baptismal Regeneration," in *International Standard Bible Encyclopedia* (Grand Rapids, MI: Eerdmans, 1939), 1:397.
9. Stephen Charnock, *The Doctrine of Regeneration* (repr. Grand Rapids, MI: Baker, 1980), 99–100.
10. Westminster Larger Catechism, Question 167.
11. John Calvin, *Treatises on the Sacraments: Catechism of the Church of Geneva, Forms of Prayer, and Confessions of Faith*, trans. Henry Beveridge (Grand Rapids, MI: Reformation Heritage, 2002), 173.

12. Richard D. Phillips, "The Lord's Supper: An Overview," in *Give Praise to God*, 197.
13. John Calvin, *The Institutes of the Christian Religion*, 2 vols. (Louisville, KY: Westminster, 1960), 2:1362 (ß4.17.2).
14. Phillips, "The Lord's Supper," 198–99.
15. Calvin, *Institutes*, 2:1370 (ß4.17.10).
16. For a fuller treatment of these passages, including a discussion of the often illegitimately appealed to John 6, see J. Ligon Duncan III, "True Communion with Christ in the Lord's Supper," in *The Westminster Confession into the 21st Century*, vol. 3 (Ross-shire: Mentor), 429–75, esp. 450–71.
17. Donald Macleod puts it forcefully: "The question of the Lord's presence in the Sacrament is not raised by the New Testament material itself" (*Priorities for the Church* [Fearn, Scotland: Christian Focus, 2003], 122).

The Gospel Coalition

The Gospel Coalition is a fellowship of evangelical churches deeply committed to renewing our faith in the gospel of Christ and to reforming our ministry practices to conform fully to the Scriptures. We have become deeply concerned about some movements within traditional evangelicalism that seem to be diminishing the church's life and leading us away from our historic beliefs and practices. On the one hand, we are troubled by the idolatry of personal consumerism and the politicization of faith; on the other hand, we are distressed by the unchallenged acceptance of theological and moral relativism. These movements have led to the easy abandonment of both biblical truth and the transformed living mandated by our historic faith. We not only hear of these influences; we see their effects. We have committed ourselves to invigorating churches with new hope and compelling joy based on the promises received by grace alone through faith alone in Christ alone.

We believe that in many evangelical churches a deep and broad consensus exists regarding the truths of the gospel. Yet we often see the celebration of our union with Christ replaced by the age-old attractions of power and affluence or by monastic retreats into ritual, liturgy, and sacrament. What replaces the gospel will never promote a mission-hearted faith anchored in enduring truth working itself out in unashamed discipleship eager to stand the tests of kingdom calling and sacrifice. We desire to advance along the King's highway, always aiming to provide gospel advocacy, encouragement, and education so that current- and next-generation church leaders are better equipped to fuel their ministries with principles and practices that glorify the Savior and do good to those for whom he shed his life's blood.

We want to generate a unified effort among all peoples—an effort that is zealous to honor Christ and multiply his disciples, joining in a true coalition for Jesus. Such a biblically grounded and united mission is the only enduring future for the church. This reality compels us to stand with others who are stirred by the conviction that the mercy of God in Jesus Christ is our only hope of eternal salvation. We desire to champion this gospel with clarity, compassion, courage, and joy—gladly linking hearts with fellow believers across denominational, ethnic, and class lines.

Our desire is to serve the church we love by inviting all of our brothers and sisters to join us in an effort to renew the contemporary church in the ancient gospel of Christ so that we truly speak and live for him in a way that clearly communicates to our age. We intend to do this through the ordinary means of his grace: prayer, the ministry of the Word, baptism and the Lord's Supper, and the fellowship of the saints. We yearn to work with all who, in addition to embracing the confession and vision set out here, seek the lordship of Christ over the whole of life with unabashed hope in the power of the Holy Spirit to transform individuals, communities, and cultures.